It Was Written In The Stars

Volume 1

Adarsh Ravi Tiwari

BookLeaf Publishing

India | USA | UK

Made with ❤ on the BookLeaf Publishing Platform
www.bookleafpub.in
www.bookleafpub.com

Dedication

To my **mom and dad**, the keepers of my dreams, and **my brother**, the light in my journey—thank you for being my greatest muses.

To all those whose stories intertwine with mine, your moments breathe life into these verses.

Poetry is my calm in all the chaos, and you are the whispers that guide me through.

Acknowledgement

First and foremost, I would like to thank my mom, dad, and brother for always being my first readers, my honest critics, and my greatest support. Your constant love, feedback, and belief in me have shaped not just my poetry, but the person I've become.

To every friend who has embraced my words and accepted my poetry from day one—thank you for your emotional and moral support. A special thank you to BookLeaf Publishing for giving me this incredible opportunity to bring my words to the world. Your trust and guidance have made this dream a reality.

I also want to express my deep gratitude to King, Talha Anjum, Talha Yunus, Jaun Elia, Rumi, and every Bollywood lyricist who has made me fall in love with words over and over again. You have been my silent mentors, teaching me the beauty of language and emotion.

Lastly, to that one heartbreak—thank you. Half of this collection wouldn't exist without the lessons learned through you

Preface

This collection of poems was born from a place deep within my mind, where overthinking often spirals into endless thoughts. Poetry became my way of channeling those tangled ideas—letting them flow from my pen into rhythmic words that give form to the chaos inside. Every poem you read here stems from the little stories I observe in the world around me, captured through my perception of life.

My relationship with poetry truly comes alive after 3 a.m., when the world is quiet, and my thoughts are at their loudest.

Since writing my first poem in 2019 to now holding this collection in my hands, it's been a journey of growth and evolution. Creating this book has become a testament to how my voice and understanding of life have transformed.

I hope you enjoy these words—some offering definitions of life, others providing a tough yet raw outlook—each a part of the rollercoaster of emotions and stories that define my world.

In the end, I just want you to find peace, as I have, in what I call my calm in all the chaos.

With Love,
Adarsh

Index

1. Chance To Redeem

i may be multi-skilled,
but i have let down 2
people,
i created a failure
thread,
it brings my life to null.

i am here because of
them,
and i couldn't fulfill one of their dreams
everyday my mirror shows my condemn,
when i am quiet, my guilt screams.

it has been a tough journey,
a tougher one for them too,
i'll try to make it worthwhile every single way,
'cause me making them proud is due.

i am trying to improve,
i thank them for another chance,
this'll be my chance to prove,
some gold medals have to be ready in

advance.

2. As Time Passed

three on the clock's
face,
i am sitting here
watching how the
world ends,
while i play Talha
Anjum's Surface,
typing a message i'll never send.

things are complicated,
can someone clear them out,
or give me life's manual instead,
because all the things have put me in doubt.

the clock struck four,
mental chaos is at an all-time high
while spotify is playing "Let Her Go,"
all the stars are also hidden in the sky.

i want to shoot out the part
the part of me which is in chaos,
but this feeling won't depart,
maybe i want a Rachel for my Ross.

3. Love < Hate

this is a tale
a tale of all emotions
mixed,
a tale of love, trust,
ego and greed,
god's plan to keep
them fixed.

love was the start,
trust became the pillar,
greed wasn't the hour's need
ego pulled them apart.

agony mixed with anger,
a combination feared by many,
for how long do they fight this war,
emotions for sale worth a penny.

this tale is like a punch to the mirror,
shattered glass showed their bond,
bleeding fists showed their loss,
a tale focusing on being fake and beyond.

4. US

the way we met,
that memory gives me
butterflies,
the way she talks,
i find myself drowning
in her eyes.

that awkwardness kills
me,
makes me want to talk
to her again and again
that smile of hers revives me,
we talk less, but we a ten on ten.

i can't believe i'm in this place again,
i don't wanna open that scar,
though i'm already waking up in love,
why does it feel perfect this time?

i know it'll be slow,
i know everyone has a past,
but i promise to love her,
i won't let her go.

5. A crime

okay why is this so tough,
why is love a crime,
haven't i suffered enough,
why do i lose every damn
time?

you made me fall for her,
you took away my friend,
it didn't matter how close
we were,
she is the prettiest poetry i penned.

i decided to stay away,
didn't want my heart to break,
now my eyes search for her every single day,
you let me make another fucking mistake.

okay love, if she's reading this,
tell her it was your mistake
maybe it was my whiskey,
or maybe i just need to take a fucking break.

6. So High

songs play in the
background,
while I sit with my
favourite person,
when the smoke heals my
wound,
memories play in tandem.

i know when my high is
gone,
i'll try to reach you,
i'll get back to the heartbreak zone,
this time the reason will be new.

why doesn't this phase go,
why do i still see my wound,
i'm at my life's all-time low,
when will my mind go sound?

can't I undo my feelings,
can't you fade away,
oh i just remembered the little things,
now i see my heart's begging you to stay.

7. Didn't We Have Fun

a feeling maybe,
like petrichor,
maybe watching
the sunset,
like the water
teasing the shore,
maybe the
combination of lipstick and cigarette.

a five-year-old maybe getting a balloon,
someone singing his heart out,
countless hours of watching the moon,
maybe driving on your favourite route.

holding your parents tight,
kissing your loved one,
watching the skyline at night,
or maybe when your love story began.

some things can't be felt,
and some are felt by everyone,
these things make my heart melt,
maybe life's all about having fun.

8. Life In A Metro

look at these small windows
everyone fighting their own
war,
why is it called the money
land,
7 islands with just one door.

everyone knows the Marine Drive,
but not the silent screams it holds,
a fight to keep yourself alive,
3 am on the clock, and all the secrets unfold.

the petrichor all year long,
the way its oceans behave,
everyone's perception of Bombay is wrong,
everyone forgets how much this city gave.

how can you romanticize Bombay,
this city never stops,
people couldn't understand it for years,
it's all about finding your calm amidst the
chaos.

9. The Great Beyond

one question left
unanswered,
what will happen to you
when you die?
you'll enjoy in heaven,
or hell will make you cry?

the toughest thing to achieve,
it is what we call *nirvana*,
the event where soul has to leave,
like permanently smoking marijuana.

yin-yang becomes real,
when your karma has to decide,
some good, some bad
it is the truth which can't hide.

no money, no humans,
achieving *moksha* is the ultimate goal,
there can't be any plans,
it comes down to the karma of your soul.

10. 3 Am Thoughts

this thought passed my mind:
why didn't she reply,
is she even fine,
or is she feeling shy?

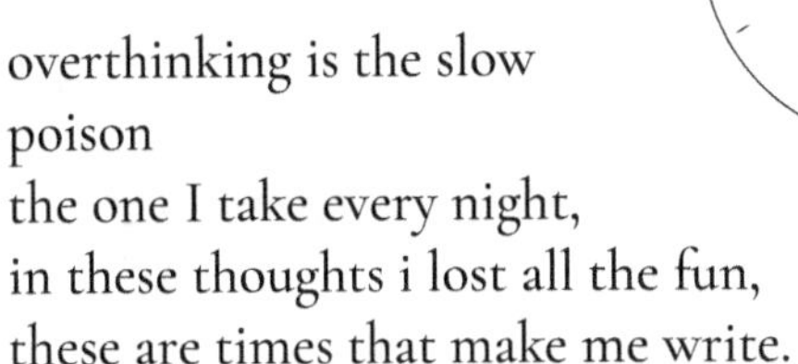

overthinking is the slow
poison
the one I take every night,
in these thoughts i lost all the fun,
these are times that make me write.

this darkness makes me think,
why do i exist,
i say, add ice to my drink,
wait life, I'll give you a list.

4 to 5 people on the road,
the ones running from the truth,
3 am is when my time slowed,
this is the setting where all the songs soothe.

welcome to life's dark mode,
it helps me stay calm,
here the thoughts in my mind explode,
this explosion is where i get my calmness
from.

11. Observations

that one lone street
light,
lighting the brightest
future to come,
here i'm sitting under 6
lights,
i don't how dark my future has become.

that one rupee coin i gave,
brought me blessings which can't be counted
here i have everything a person can have,
i don't even remember the last good thing i
said.

someone riding a kayak in the ocean,
here i'm sitting in the Titanic,
lost in a perfect world,
i don't even know my reason for panic.

someone in love saying the cringiest thing,
here i'm writing this at one,
maybe being emotionless is cringe,
i don't even know what i've become.

12. Priorities

what are priorities, i ask,
why am i sitting here
insecure,
why do people have to
prove their love,
why am i waking up
unsure?

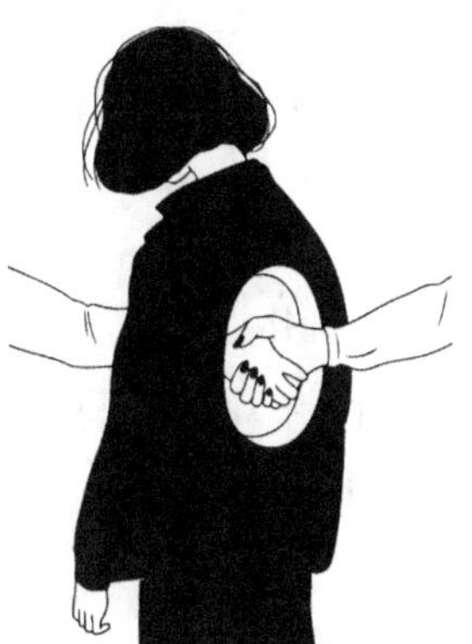

that Instagram story i
wasn't a part of,
does it deserve to affect me,
if i act all mature,
why am i writing this at three?

why can't i understand,
change is the only fucking constant,
why am i acting like sheldon,
why is my mood always to rant?

slowly and surely i'll change,
maybe i don't need to find a way,
maybe i'll always remember the saying:
'those who love you, will stay.'

13. Can't Handle

there are poems
inside you,
that paper can't
handle,
there are words
inside you,
that people can't
handle.

i may have written a hundred pieces,
there's one poem i can't handle
i may not care about anyone,
but her tears i can't handle.

there is hate around you,
that your heart can't handle,
there is pain around you,
that your mind can't handle.

there is love around me,
that my poetry can't handle,
and there is me with you,
that the universe can't handle.

14. Part of My Dreams

i want to make a
mistake
i want to get my heart
broken,
i want to take a break,
i want to fall in love
again.

i have a lot of feelings unshared,
my eyes are stuck on a girl,
the saved love memes thread,
i share it and my heart takes a whirl.

i talk to her once in a while,
she shares some funny things,
her message brings me a smile,
this feeling isn't like the flings.

i know it's not meant to be,
but what's the harm in savouring dreams,
i know how loved she'll be,
but it's just a matter of sharing some memes.

15. Question Mark

what if i didn't feel
anything,
all the emotions lost,
what if i stopped
listening to king,
all the happy thoughts
exhaust?

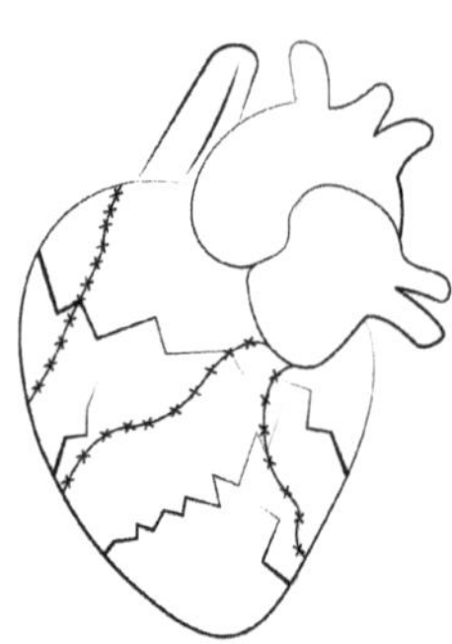

what if i stopped writing
poetry,
all my thoughts pile up,
what if i stopped liking the sky,
had no replies for 'sup'?

what if music isn't there,
my mind gets confused,
what if there's no one to care,
for me heaven's entry is refused?

what if the long drives stop,
i have nothing to do,
what if my books flop,
can i do something new?

16. Questions

where is my mind
lost,
why do our
memories not
fade,
why am i on the
road of frost,
where is the boy who wasn't afraid?

why do countless hours pass,
why am i in a fix
is my heart made of glass,
why am i writing this at six?

why did i let her go,
why is everything hurting me,
why aren't things going in a flow,
why isn't my mind free?

why am i not liking anything,
why are things in chaos
why am i acting like Chandler Bing,
why am i as lonely as Ross?

17. Death

a reality no one has seen,
one that is feared the
most,
a part of life's routine,
something you don't
wanna boast.

lust, love, envy, greed,
pride,
nothing will matter if you have this,
this never favours a side,
oh baby, it'll let you reminisce.

people who love you will cry,
though it will fade a month after you leave,
you'll get your fame when you die,
and a new pattern will itself weave.

few days ago, i found death to be heavenly,
but some newspapers changed that for me,
i feel it's the beginning of the end,
i can't even listen to it, what a fighter she
must be.

18. Young / Old

the child in me,
wants to play games all day,
but the adult me,
is too tired to play.

the child in me,
wants a huge group of
friends,
but the adult me,
wants only two clowns as the day ends.

the child in me,
wants to have infinite beers in bars,
but the adult me,
wants whiskey with ice while gazing at the
stars.

the child in me,
can run away from problems, big or small
but the adult me,
has to stand up and face them all.

19. The Race

watching her fade away,
slowly winning the race,
the one to see who quits
first,
watching her ruin my
happy place.

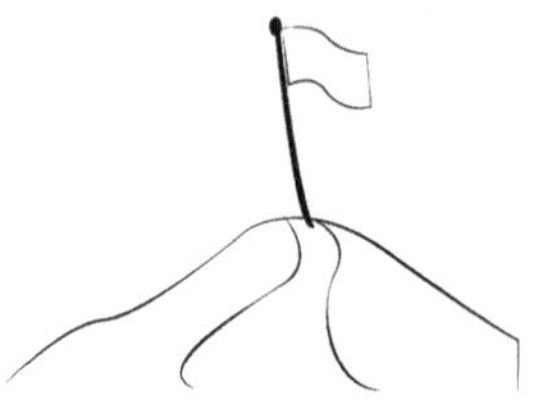

are we oddly satisfied by loneliness,
or do we all have a beating rock,
are we too scared to fall in love,
why am i writing this at 4 o'clock?

maybe she hurt me today,
maybe she always does,
why do i find comfort in being numb,
why isn't love the way it was?

4 am and the demons in my head,
made me forget how beautiful she is,
maybe no one will quit,
it's just the overthinking that hurts.

20. Apocalypse

the way you look,
the way you smile,
like the smell of a new
book,
please stay for a while?

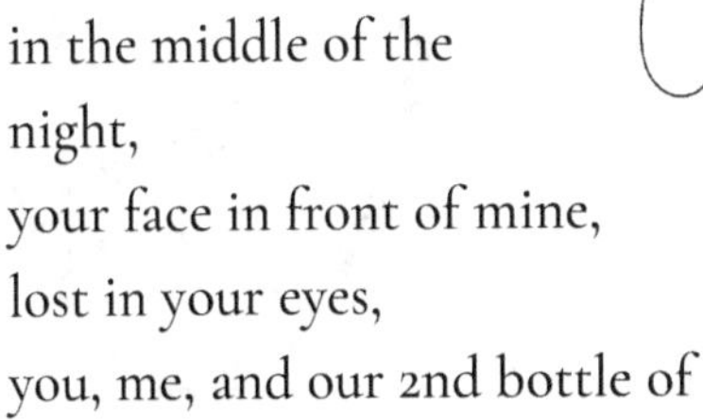

in the middle of the
night,
your face in front of mine,
lost in your eyes,
you, me, and our 2nd bottle of wine.

lost in Coldplay's paradise,
our lips cause an apocalypse,
all our stress lost in the smoke,
ours is a little boat in an ocean full of ships.

there's a problem though—
why is it just a dream,
leave your address when you go,
i hope when i find you, all is as it seems.

21. Mindset

hold on to the ones you
love,
as time is destined to
change,
the answer always is
not all of the above,
distance from the ones
acting strange.

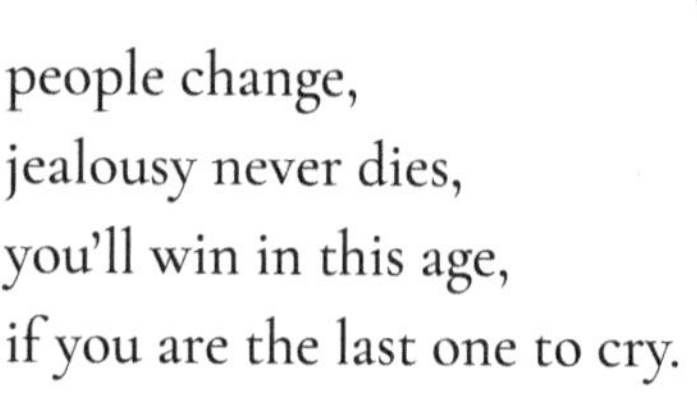

people change,
jealousy never dies,
you'll win in this age,
if you are the last one to cry.

fakeness all around,
how are we supposed to hide,
being real has just become a sound,
all the goodwill is dead inside.

one for family, one for friends
three faces with the mask,
what is the need for two faces,
is the toughest question one can be asked.

22. Don't Come

how have you been?
my heart is trying to
figure it out,
maybe our story
wasn't worth it,
my mind is still in
doubt.

the day you left,
i decided to burn
your pictures,
last night when i played our song,
the ashes slipped out of my palm.

maybe i loved you in a rush
maybe i don't know you yet,
i hope i made a mistake,
you were the reason of my first cigarette.

i never hope you come back,
i'll be rude if you do,
i would have to knock myself out,
'cause no one can be rude to you.

23. With A Diamond Spoon

born with a diamond
spoon,
never knew what hardships
were,
everything was served to
him on a plate,
never knew people had to
fight their own wars.

waking up to love everyday,
never knew how it feels to lose,
all the stars were aligned for him,
never knew the meaning of Monday blues.

looks like a fairy tale,
life would be good in his shoes,
no one knows the hardships he faced,
he lives a life no one would choose.

there is love for him,
but there's nothing to fill his void
everything looks perfect for him,
but his inner voice seems destroyed

24. Unexplainable

pain that Gulzaar
couldn't write, 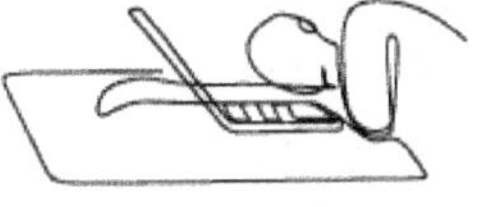
laughter brought tears to
eyes,
sadness which made even Anjum high,
love that Rumi couldn't define.

no amount of alcohol could help,
the pain was unbearable,
laughed at his mistakes,
that man wasn't stable.

he didn't come this far—
this far only to lose,
but he was defeated by his own voices,
next step was going to be drug abuse.

sadness wasn't a feeling,
it became his comfort place,
the voices made him fall in love,
there was a picture he couldn't erase....

25. Happy Zone

maybe the first eye
contact,
maybe the smile on
her face,
maybe her head on
my shoulder—
how can someone be the definition of grace?

yes, these are the things i dream of,
yes, it's my happy zone
either i fear love,
or i've fought too much alone.

why isn't it okay to feel things,
why is being alone a trend,
maybe i'm stuck with the wrong people,
why aren't love stories being penned?

the search for that someone might end
someday,
maybe i'll have a companion at war,
i don't know if they'll be here to stay,
or if it'll become a famous lore.

26. As Pure As A Reflection

she was beautiful,
as beautiful as the sunshine,
as Anuv jain's gul,
a creation, as fine as wine.

he was madly in love,
in love with her smile,
it looked like a movie from above,
something as deep as the nile.

they couldn't be separated,
they had decided to stay,
their bond was like a holy thread,
which couldn't be broken in any way.

fate had decided something else for them;
it decided to bring it to an end,
but their love was so pure that fate was in
condemn,
 but for them, even fate had to bend.

27. Neural Coordination

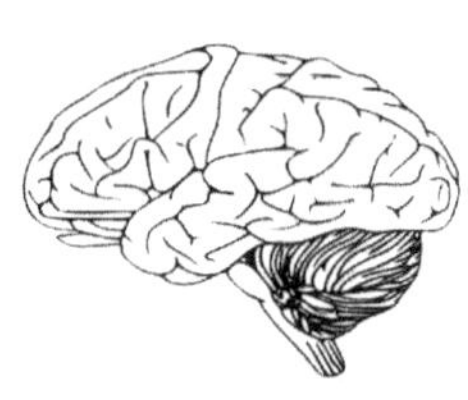

my heart shouts at me,
a coward can't do
anything,
my brain tells me to
see,
the possibility of
ruining everything.

my heart shouts at me—
'go tell her everything you feel!'
my brain tells me to be free,
and wonders if everything is real?

my heart shouts at me—
'if you don't tell her, how will she know?'
my brain convinces me,
to just take it slow.

my heart shouts at me,
though i know it is wrong,
my brain tells me to disagree,
but heart is where all my emotions belong.

28. Paracosm

the place where there's
love,
where i'll smile all the
time,
where i have a roof
above,
a place with no crime.

a place with Bombay's rain,
a place which has winters like Delhi,
where i'll party like it's Ibiza in Spain,
and have momos in my belly.

a place with a Marine Drive,
where a woman can go out at night,
a place where music is alive,
while its beauty helps me write.

this has been a *sweven*,
where i speak to the aurora,
this will be my personal heaven,
the place which matches my aura.

29. Managing People

yes, i saw her again,
how do i explain it to my
friends,
maybe she is the one i'll love,
maybe sad is not the only way
it ends.

coffee with her, or,
whiskey with my constants,
how do i tell them,
i'm having the best time with my parents.

i really wanna sit with you mom,
how do i tell my brother to wait,
i really need to get back to my studies,
how do i expain why i slept at 6 and woke at
8?

why is managing people so difficult,
or am i not getting things straight,
how do i tell the woman i like,
she needs to wait...

30. Melancholic

my eyes are open wide
still i'm dreaming,
it's the middle of the night,
hey sleep? come meet me.

feeling everything at once,
but there's nothing to
elaborate,
maybe one less glass of rum,
at least i won't blame my fate.

this melancholic behaviour,
isn't something new,
i at least want a reason to be sad,
but i have no clue.

hoping the stars to align,
maybe this time to free my mind,
looking for the universe's sign,
just to leave the melancholy behind.

31. No Alcohol

i saw the rain pouring down,
heard the voices in my head
getting louder,
thought about running out
of town,
fuck the absolute, imma need something
stronger.

my scotch glass full of ice,
her face constant on my mind,
tears fall stronger than ever from my eyes,
all our memories making me blind.

the phone dial pad is up,
my voices want to make a call,
should i just drop a 'supp'
or give it my all?

i surely messed up my talisker,
i shouldn't have messed someone else's mind
too,
why did i have to say hi to her,
what have i gotten myself into?

32. 9<——>5

you wake up and
follow it,
the same drive,
the same routine,
your favourite nine to five.

with a max load of caffeine,
a fucked cycle of sleep,
crush's messages left on seen,
google showing alcohol for cheap.

come back to staple dal rice,
the odd hours of five to nine,
calling best friend for advice,
with anger-filled thoughts to resign

you wake up and follow it,
this time the artist's routine,
writing, singing, and the will to stay fit,
penning life and goals with the monotony in
between.

33. Fight

ever got your heart broken?
ever felt a chapter of life close
without an end?
felt defeated again and again?
all this while, did you
pretend?

problems can be countless,
your win is what matters,
listen more, speak less,
the stress is here for a week,
your actions for years.

let go of that pain,
it's okay to let that boat sink,
break your traumatic chain,
fuck it and grab your drink.

your parents raised you right,
some losers can't change that,
get up and win this fight,
mentally or straight-up in Mortal Kombat.

34. Thread

ever felt a loss?
a pause in your life,
a lost coin toss,
your back with a
knife?

i am numb without a reason,
a change i can't process,
fuck it's the 6th glass of rum
i still don't know how to clear this mess.

times are changing,
why the fuck don't i get that,
why do i wanna be stuck in a loop,
why am i still wearing the nostalgic hat?

is it me being immature,
or the voices in my head
is it my loneliness,
i hope it doesn't break my only thread.

35. Constant

what is a defeat,
why is it letting me
drown,
why did i lose my
seat,
when did i keep my
guard down?

loss after loss after loss,
are my words hurting people,
mornings are okay
nights have become absolutely dull.

why does everyone go away,
tell me how to please you,
it's fucked up every day,
just the reasons are new.

36. Poets

like it when they are
alone,
owners of their work,
love whatever writings
they own,
look at some lines and
smirk.

we are present in a huge amount,
we all have millions of lines,
infinite poems one cannot count,
different words put in different designs.

poetry i feel is a superpower,
it helps us show a different perception,
we can be active at different hours,
our words can create any deception.

if i write everything about us,
a chamber of secrets will be revealed,
let it be hidden and let's not discuss,
the amount of power we wield...

37. Can It Be Aeonian?

i gave you part of me,
the part that kept me free
ask yourself what you did with it,
rewind life's tape and you shall
see.

seeing you was the highlight of the day,
like seeing the sky during a sunset,
but you couldn't stay,
how can one forget?

i know this wasn't a relationship,
but it was the most beautiful feeling,
this felt like a crazy trip,
but its end is from what my heart is healing.

i feel like a rockstar's Jordan,
where you are my heer,
like Ranjhana's kundan,
you are Zoya and i am just waiting to see her.

giving you a part of me was tough,
i don't even know if we'll talk again,
i think my suffering has been enough,
just come back and we'll be in love then.

38. That Someone

someone to take that
one walk,
that one kiss,
someone with whom i
talk,
someone i'll miss.

someone to have that
coffee,
with whom i'll watch friends,
someone for whom i'll bring a toffee,
with whom my day ends.

someone i'll take along on a long drive
with whom i visit all the bars,
with whom i'll watch Coldplay perform live,
someone with whom i'll gaze at the stars,

i hope i find this someone soon,
with whom i listen to my favourite playlists,
to whom i can promise to bring the moon,
whom i'll love till my life exists.

39. Away from Lies

i don't miss you anymore,
but whenever i watch a
sunset,
i remember your laughs
from before
just like the time we first
met.

i have tried forgetting you,
but my heart stops me,
i don't know what i have gotten myself into.
now time shall only see.

i see every hour pass,
looking at the sky
was your heart made of glass?
i ask this with tears in my eyes,

music will help me rise,
and it will keep me away from her
my soul is just done with your lies,
but i still miss the vibe you were.

40. Like The Oceans

i have an obsession,
which is coloured in you,
smoother than Coldplay's fun,
who doesn't love the colour
blue?

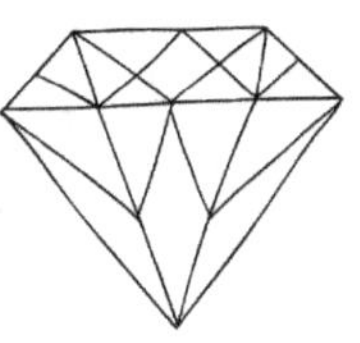

blue hair curled,
or as you see the sky,
with the domination in this world,
blue colour has a different high.

the woman i love has blue eyes,
it isn't a colour but an expression of life
this hue has a lot of lies,
yet this is used to cancel all the strife.

known as the colour of peace,
this has been my favourite forever,
this for me is a special piece
blue, in my mind is a treasure.

41. A Broken Man

i guess i'll never find
a way,
one that'll help me
find myself,
a man who was left
broken that day,
is fighting to find
himself.

beautiful lies surely broke me,
but i wanna skip to the good part,
oh fuck, the clock struck three,
another sleepless night is tearing me apart.

i feel incomplete,
i want someone to complete me,
i don't know when we will meet,
what if she's already there and i can't see?

42. Beautiful Lies

you said that you
loved him
he took it in earnest,
'cause we know trust
is key,
but the first thing he
lost was trust.

you told him you couldn't live without him
he thought he was loved,
but he found himself feeling grim,
your lies had him shoved.

you told him all your dreams,
he made them his to achieve,
your lies took him to new extremes,
i had never seen a boy this broken and naive.

you told him all the lies,
but his love for you increased everyday,
he thought there was love in your eyes,
your lies left him broken in a different way.

43. What Is Love?

a feeling above
everything,
many have given up
living for this,
it can be long or just a
fling,
love is something as pure as bliss.

millions of thoughts around it,
no person can deny its need,
it's your karma and destiny well-knit,
love is like being high on weed.

thinking about them all day,
someone you'll genuinely miss,
a feeling in which everyone wants to stay,
love is something that'll let you have your
first kiss.

being in it is not necessary,
you can try living without it,
maybe your mind is contrary,
as love is like a euphoric hit.

44. Parallel Universe

suddenly the sky meant
nothing,
stars didn't make me smile
love was nothing more than
a fling,
hoodies were out of style.

suddenly Bombay closed at
ten,
my showers were 5 minutes long,
everyone wasn't confused again,
all my feelings were wrong.

suddenly i had that someone,
gen-z songs started making sense then,
everyone woke up with the sun,
my thoughts were normal again.

i hope this doesn't come true,
how will my tears wash away in the shower,
how will i miss you,
how will i overthink at the midnight hour.

45. Let The Eyes Talk

let the eyes talk,
they have a lot to say,
go into them, take a walk,
you'll be begging to stay.

love, i guess, often fades,
whether it's Romeo and
Juliet,
it has a lot of shades,
love is the thing people
often forget.

you have someone or you don't,
love is what everyone needs,
being alone is not what people want,
life is a thread and love is one of its beads.

there was someone in my life too,
i loved her with all of me,
my broken heart was nothing new
still i ask the stars every day, how is she?

46. Our Eyes Were Closed

life is the calm that
everyone craves,
we think we will sink,
but it has its own waves
it turns into chaos in a
blink.

was our meeting fate,
or a beautiful mistake,
my heart didn't get that straight,
or maybe it wasn't awake.

us meeting was elysian,
like soil meeting the land,
like a different kind of adhesion,
or a mistake well planned.

we stood hand in hand,
through life's highs and lows
although we were broken to stand,
amidst it all, our eyes had to close.....

47. Oneiromancy

she had the viridity,
she was as pretty as the
stars,
was she from my city,
or was she a quasar?

her eyes had that one
thing,
like the moon's
reflection on water,
she could even sing,
it was as if the gods
had brought her.

she was wearing a black dress,
and she was laconic,
she was looking like a princess,
with a drink of gin and water which was tonic

her vibes were serene,
like the sound of the waves,
yet her eyes also showed pain,
perhaps love is what she craves?

48. City Lights

Sparkles from the top,
the LEDs are in a cluster,
It's dark when they stop,
it has to be city lights with
me and her.

according to some people,
Hong Kong has the best
skyline,
but your own terrace is the best place, i feel,
city lights are a feeling as fine as wine.

drive to the Queen's necklace,
you'll see Mumbai's finest skyline,
it is a beautiful place,
the place where even the water shines.

there's a concrete jungle we live in,
city lights make it bearable,
it has been with Nature through thick and
thin,
they make a connection so pretty and stable.

49. Being Lonely

this feeling of being
lonely,
it can be a slow poison
for some,
i have experienced it very
closely,
it makes the soul of a
person numb.

it is like having blank pages,
which can be filled but no one does it,
it has its own stages,
it is like having a permanent hit.

but i feel being lonely is better,
than having a fake friend
if you are lonely, write a letter,
because someday this feeling will end.

when you find that 'someone,' it'll end,
try not to slip back into that phase,
if you do, try finding that letter you penned,
and let all the memories play from those days.

50. Like Stars Miss The Sky

i'll miss you,
like the stars miss the
sky,
you left my heart in two,
i wish it were all a lie.

losing someone you love,
teaches you to be brave,
is there really a better place above,
or is the end nothing more than a grave?

questions will always remain unanswered,
it is always the decision of fate,
a wise man once said,
we all have to be there, some early, some late.

i am obviously sitting in lies,
i'll always believe you are fine,
i'll try playing all our memories,
you have crossed it, i'll also try crossing life's
end line.

(last one had to be for you, putu, imy)